Breakfast Meals

Ham and Egg Pies

Ingredients

1 teaspoon olive oil

12 slices ham (thin)

12 eggs

12 cherry tomatoes

1 tablespoon chives, finely chopped 2 tablespoons parmesan cheese, grated

Directions

First of all, oil a TWELVE holes muffin pan.

After this, use the ham slice for lining the molds.

After this, break an egg into every hollow, use tomato for topping Scatter the items like, chives, parmesan, salt as well as pepper all over, Then bake at THREE HUNDRED FIFTY (35o) degrees Fahrenheit for approximately 1/3 hour or till egg is set.

Then take out of oven and allow to cool for FIVE min.

Vegemite on Toast

Ingredients

2 slices bread, preferable white

1/8 teaspoon vegemite, more if you are game

1/2 teaspoon butter or 1/2 teaspoon margarine

Directions

First of all, toast a bread and butter it.

Then after this, spread a fine layer of vegemite over it.

Banana Nut Bread

Ingredients

3 cups flour

3/4 teaspoon salt

1 teaspoon baking soda 2 cups sugar

1 teaspoon cinnamon

3 eggs

1 cup oil

2 cups mashed bananas (ripe) 1 (8 ounce) cans crushed pineapple with juice 1 teaspoon vanilla

1/2-1 cup chopped walnuts

Directions

First of all, blend the eggs, oil and sugar in a bowl.

Then add the remaining items besides nuts and blend well.

Then blend in nuts.

Bake for approximately 1 hour at THREE HUNDRED FIFTY (35o) degrees Fahrenheit or till ready and done.

Breakfast on an English Muffin

Ingredients

4 English muffins or 8 crumpets, cut in half 1/3 cup peanut butter

1/3 cup honey

2 bananas, thinly sliced

1/8 teaspoon cinnamon

Directions

First of all, slightly toast the muffins.

Take peanut butter and spread this over the muffins.

Then spread honey over the muffins.

Use the bananas for topping.

Then grill till honey sizzles.

Use cinnamon as sprinkle.

Cinnamon and Raisin Oats

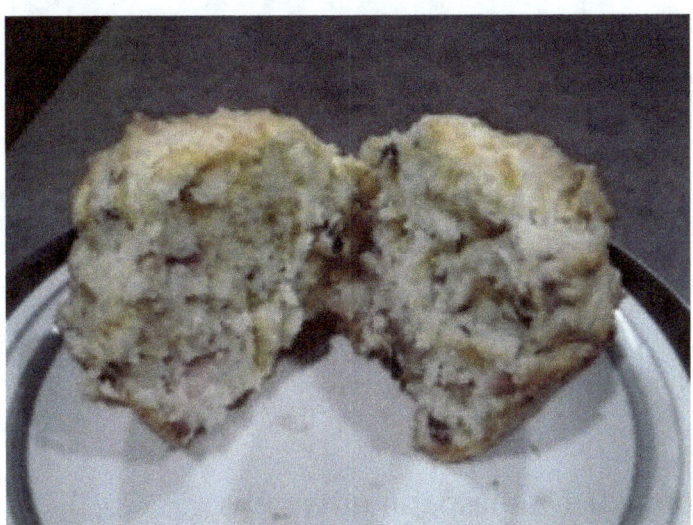

Ingredients

250 ml skim milk (1 cup) 1 tablespoon sugar

45 g instant oats (1/2 cup) 1 1/2 tablespoons raisins 1/2 teaspoon cinnamon ground cinnamon, extra to serve (optional)

Directions

Take the milk and mix it with sugar in saucepan and heat to boiling over moderate temperature.

Blend in oats. Blend in raisins. Blend in cinnamon.

Cook, mixing from time to time, for THREE min or till become thick.

Then distribute into bowls and use additional cinnamon as sprinkle.

Cheese & Bacon Breakfast Muffins

Ingredients

3 slices bacon (rind removed and chopped) 1 tablespoon olive oil

400 g button mushrooms (finely chopped) 1 1/2 cups plain flour

3 teaspoons baking powder

1/4 teaspoon salt (freshly ground) 1/4 teaspoon black pepper (freshly ground) 1 cup cheese (grated)

2 tablespoons chives (finely chopped) 80 g butter (melted)

2 eggs (lightly whisked)

2/3 cup milk

Directions

First of all, sauté the bacon over moderately high temperature setting in sauté pan till golden in color, mixing from time to time.

Then shift to paper towel.

Add the oil and mushrooms to sauté pan and cook for FIVE min over high temperature setting till soft.

Then put aside.

Grease a TWELVE holes muffin tin.

Take the flour, baking powder and sift these items with salt and pepper in a bowl and then add in cheese.

Then add in chives and blend them well.

Take the butter and whisk with egg and milk in jug and pour this over dry items, mixing till mixed.

Then right after this, fold through bacon and mushrooms.

Take mixture and spoon this into pan.

Bake for approximately 1/3 hour at TWO HUNDRED (2oo) degrees Celsius.

Pacific Style Omelet

Ingredients

6 large eggs

1 medium potato, grated

1 tablespoon parsley, diced 100 g ham, Virginian sliced and diced 1/4 teaspoon ground black pepper 1/4 teaspoon sage

1 medium onion, finely diced 1 tablespoon butter

2 button mushrooms, sliced 2 cherry tomatoes, sliced 1/4 green capsicum, diced (green pepper) 1/4 red capsicum, diced (red pepper) 2 teaspoons parmesan cheese 100 g cream cheese, finely diced

Directions

Take the eggs and whisk them in bowl.

Take the grated potato, onion, sage, parsley, ham, pepper and add them to bowl and blend them.

Add the mixture to melted butter in pan over moderate temperature so it begin bubbling.

Take the mushrooms, tomato, cheese, capsicum and spread them over.

Cook for approximately ½ hour or till top begins to get firm.

Chop in half, don't fold.

Lemonade Scones

Ingredients

1 cup heavy cream
1 cup lemonade
3 cups self-rising flour 1 pinch salt
jam, to serve
cream, to serve

Directions

Blend everything together in a bowl.

Then knead and shape the dough out to approximately ONE inch thick.

After this, chop out scones by using round shape cutter.

Then put them on cookie sheet that has been greased.

Use milk for brushing the tops.

Then bake for approximately ¼ hour at FOUR HUNDRED FIFTY (45o) degrees Fahrenheit or till top become brown in color.

You can serve this delicious recipe with cream and jam.

Asparagus Omelette Wraps

Ingredients

8 eggs

1/2 cup milk

1 tablespoon fresh sage, roughly chopped 1 teaspoon fresh thyme, chopped 2 garlic cloves, chopped 1/4 cup pecorino cheese, grated 24 stalks asparagus

2 tablespoons extra virgin olive oil

Directions

Take eggs and beat them in bowl.

Take milk, sage and add them to bowl along with pecorino, garlic and thyme.

Then use the cracked black pepper for seasoning.

After this, layer the asparagus in pan with enough salted and boiling water in order to cover spears.

Cook for 120 seconds till soft however yet crunchy.

After this, pour a ladle of egg mixture in little bit heated olive oil in heated sauté pan and roll the pan around till egg is finely layered over base and cooked on one side.

Then lower the temperature and turn over to cook egg on the 2nd side.
Use the asparagus for filling the crepes.

Crumpets With Cheese & Bacon

Ingredients

4 crumpets

1/4 cup cheddar cheese, grated

50 g bacon (one large slice or rasher) 1/4 teaspoon ground pepper (optional) 1/4 teaspoon ground paprika (optional)

Directions

First of all, cook the bacon in skillet and put aside.

Use the cheese as sprinkle all over every crumpet and then sprinkle the pepper and paprika.

Then after this, tear up the bacon and put over top and remove the fat and rind.

Then grill for approximately TEN min or till cheese melts into crumpet.

Main Dish Meals

Basil Cream Chicken

Ingredients

hot cooked and drained fettuccine 1 lb boneless skinless chicken breast, cubed 1 cup minced onion

3/4 lb fresh mushrooms, sliced 2 tablespoons oil

3 tablespoons butter

3 tablespoons flour

2 cups chicken broth

1 tablespoon chicken bouillon 1 cup whipping cream

2 tablespoons minced fresh basil 1/4 teaspoon pepper

Directions

Take the chicken, mushrooms, onions and fry them in oil for FOUR min.

Blend in flour in melted butter in saucepan till become smooth.

Then add in chicken broth. Add in boullion. Add in cream.

Blend in basil. Blend in pepper.

Heat to boiling, cook and mix for 120 seconds.

Mix with chicken mixture.

You can serve this delicious recipe over fettuccini.

Chicken Stew

Ingredients

1/4 cup oil

1 cup chopped onion

1 (14 ounce) cans diced tomatoes 2 cups chicken broth

1 teaspoon minced garlic 1 teaspoon thyme

1 bay leaf

1 teaspoon salt

1/2 teaspoon pepper

4 cups diced potatoes

1 1/2 cups sliced carrots 2 cups chopped chicken breasts

Directions

Fry the onion in oil in pot for 120 seconds.

Add the following SEVEN items.

Heat to boiling.

Take potatoes, chicken, carrots and add them.

Allow to simmer till veggies are ready and done, approximately ½ hour.

Use the cornstarch for thickening the stew.

Super Delicious Grilled Salmon

Ingredients

2 -8 salmon steaks or 2 -8 chicken breasts 1/2 cup peanut oil

4 tablespoons soy sauce

4 tablespoons balsamic vinegar 1/2 onion, chopped

1 tablespoon brown sugar 2 garlic cloves, minced

1 1/2 teaspoons fresh ginger, grated 1 teaspoon crushed red pepper flakes 1 teaspoon sesame oil

1/2 teaspoon salt

Directions

First of all, prepare marinade from sesame oil, peanut oil, soy sauce, salt, red pepper flakes, vinegar, ginger, onions, garlic, and brown sugar in Ziploc bag.

Mix well and insert chicken or fish and seal the bag.

Allow to marinate in refrigerator for FOUR TO TWENTY FOUR hrs.

Then grill the fish on moderately high temperature setting for FIVE min each side or till fish flakes easily.

Parmesan Crusted Broiled Scallops

Ingredients

1/3 cup finely crushed onion flavored melba toast, about 9

1 tablespoon grated parmesan cheese 1 tablespoon minced fresh parsley 1/4 teaspoon paprika

1 1/2 lbs sea scallops

1 tablespoon butter, melted lemon wedge

Directions

Mix the 1st FOUR items and ONE FOURTH tsp of black pepper in Ziploc plastic bag.

Use the butter for brushing the scallops.

Then add them to bag and seal the bag and shake well.

Put the scallops on broiler pan sprayed with cooking oil.

Then broil for TEN min or till ready and done.

You can serve this delicious recipe with lemon wedges.

Easy Pork Chops

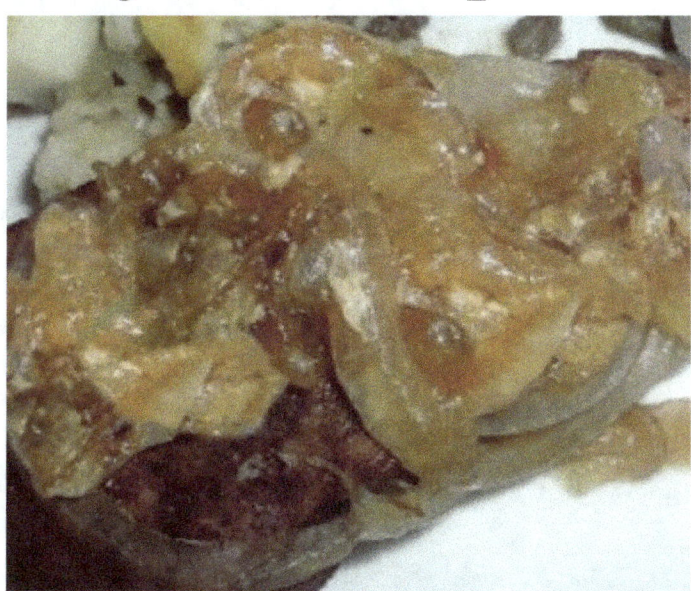

Ingredients

1/2 teaspoon salt

1/4 teaspoon pepper

1/4 teaspoon paprika

1/4 teaspoon sage

1/4 teaspoon thyme

4 boneless pork loin chops 1 tablespoon oil

1 onion, sliced

Directions

Blend dry items and sprinkle on each of the side of pork chops.

After this, cook the chops in oil.

Then put every chop on heavy foil piece.

After this, layer each one with onions.

After this, seal the pouches.

Then put on baking sheet.

Finally, bake for ½ hour at FOUR HUNDRED TWENTY FIVE (425) degrees Fahrenheit.

Crock Pot Chuck Roast With Vegetables

Ingredients

1 1/2 cups sliced carrots 1 cup chopped onion

1 cup sliced celery

4 potatoes, cut in chunks 3 lbs boneless chuck roast 1 envelope onion soup mix 1 (10 ounce) cans condensed golden mushroom soup 2 cups water

1 tablespoon horseradish

Directions

Put veggies in pot in mentioned order.

After this, put roast on veggies.

Blend the rest of items together.

Then pour over the roast.

Cook for FIVE hrs on high temperature setting.

Tasty Herb Roasted Turkey

Ingredients

1 (14 ounce) cans chicken broth 3 tablespoons lemon juice 1 teaspoon basil

1 teaspoon thyme

1/2 teaspoon garlic salt 1/4 teaspoon pepper

1/4 teaspoon poultry seasoning 12 -14 lbs turkey

Directions

Blend all of the basting items.

Put the turkey in roaster pan.

Then roast the turkey at THREE HUNDRED TWENTY FIVE (325) degrees Fahrenheit.

Use broth mixture for basting the chicken each 30 min.

Turkey is going to be ready and done in FOUR TO FIVE hrs.

Spinach and Mandarin Orange Salad

Ingredients

8 cups torn spinach

8 ounces sliced fresh mushrooms 2 (11 ounce) cans mandarin orange sections, in light syrup or in own juice, drained 1/4 cup crumbled blue cheese or 1/4 cup crumbled feta cheese 2 tablespoons roughly chopped pecans or 2 tablespoons roughly chopped walnuts 1/2 cup fat-free raspberry vinaigrette

Directions

Put two cups spinach on each of the FOUR dishes.

Organize half cup of mushrooms and ONE THIRD cup of oranges over the spinach.

Use one tbsp of cheese and 1.5 tsp of nuts as sprinkles all over every serving.

Then use two tbsp of vinaigrette to drizzle over each serving.

Lentil and Pea Soup

Ingredients

1 tablespoon vegetable oil

1 1/2 cups chopped Spanish onions 1 1/2 teaspoons garlic, minced 12 cups water

1 cup dried brown lentils

1 cup dried split peas

4 smoked ham hocks (about 3 3/4 lbs) 1 tablespoon salt

1 tablespoon lemon juice

1/2 teaspoon dried thyme leaves 1/2 teaspoon dried sage

1/2 teaspoon dried marjoram

1 -2 bay leaf

1 1/2 cups diced carrots

1 1/4 cups chopped celery

lemon slice

Directions

Fry the garlic and onion in oil in dutch oven over moderate temperature for FIVE min, mixing till tender.

Add the rest of items besides lemon slices, carrots and celery.

Heat to boiling.

Lower the temperature and cover the pot.

Allow to simmer for approximately 75 min.
Add in carrots. Add in celery.
Heat back to boiling then lower the temperature.
Allow to simmer, for ¾ hour.
Take the pot away from heat.
After this, take out the hocks and bay leaf. Then remove the bay leaves.
Allow to cool the hocks and remove the bones and fat.
Place the meat back in soup and blend and heat.
After this, float a lemon slice over every serving.

One Dish Meals

Crock Pot Creamy Pacific Chicken

Ingredients

4 -6 boneless skinless chicken breasts, halved 1 (1 1/4 ounce) envelopes dried salad dressing mix 2 ounces water

8 ounces cream cheese, softened

1 (10 1/2 ounce) cans reduced-sodium cream of chicken soup, undiluted 1 (4 ounce) cans mushroom stems and pieces, drained hot cooked rice or pasta

Directions

Take chicken breast halves and put them in crock pot.

Take the dressing mix and blend it with water till become smooth.

After this, pour this over the chicken.

Cook, covered, on low temperature setting for THREE hrs.

Take the cream cheese and mix it with soup till become smooth.

Blend in mushroom pieces.

Take the soup mixture and pour this over the chicken.

Cook for next 60 min or till chicken is cooked through.

You can serve this delicious recipe over the cooked rice.

Beef Stew Crock Pot Style

Ingredients

1 cup sun-dried tomatoes, not packed in oil or 1 cup use 1 can diced tomatoes (14.5 ounce) or 1 (1 1/2 ounce) cans stewed tomatoes 1 1/2 lbs beef stew meat

12 potatoes, medium, cut in half (1 1/2 lbs) 1 medium onion, cut into 8 wedges 1 (8 ounce) bags baby carrots (about 30) 2 cups water

1 1/2 teaspoons seasoning salt 1 bay leaf

1/4 cup water

2 tablespoons all-purpose flour

Directions

First of all, rehydrate the tomatoes as instructed on the package, drain and then chop them coarsely.

Take the tomatoes and blend them with rest of items besides ONE FOURTH cup of water and flour in crock pot slow cooker.

Cook, covered, on low temperature for EIGHT TO NINE hrs or till vegetables and beef become soft.

Take ONE FOURTH cup of water and whisk with flour and blend into beef mixture.

Cook, covered crock pot on high temperature for ¼ hour extra.

Discard the bay leaf.

Grilled Salmon

Ingredients

8 (4 ounce) salmon fillets

1/2 cup peanut oil

4 tablespoons balsamic vinegar 4 tablespoons lemon juice

4 tablespoons green onions, chopped 4 tablespoons soy sauce

1 tablespoon brown sugar

1 1/2 teaspoons ground ginger 1 teaspoon paprika

1 teaspoon pepper

1 teaspoon crushed red pepper flakes 1 teaspoon salt

1 teaspoon sesame oil

4 garlic cloves, minced

Directions

Take the peanut oil, balsamic vinegar and blend them together with lemon juice, green onions, brown sugar, soy sauce, garlic cloves, sesame oil, ginger, paprika, salt, pepper and pepper flakes in a bowl.

Then mix the salmon fillets with the marinate.

Then keep, covered, in refrigerator for TWO TO TWENTY FOUR hrs.

Orange Pork Chops

Ingredients

2 pork chops, trimmed

1 tablespoon extra virgin olive oil 1 sweet potatoes or 1 yam, peeled 1 orange, cut in half, one half in slices the other half left whole 1 dash cinnamon

salt

cayenne pepper

Directions

First of all, cook the chops in oil.

After this, squeeze juice of half orange all over the pork chops.

While you are cooking the chops deglaze the pan.

Then chop the sweet potato into slices.

Take the meat, sweet potato slices, juice and put them in baking dish.

Use the cinnamon as sprinkle along with salt, and cayenne pepper.

Cover with the slices of orange.

Finally, bake for 60 min, covered, at THREE HUNDRED FIFTY (35o) degrees Fahrenheit or till meat become soft.

Delicious Eggs

Ingredients

1 lb bacon, cooked and crumbled 1 1/2 cups shredded cheese

6 eggs, beaten slightly

2 cups milk

2 7/8 ounces fried onions

sour cream, for garnish

chopped chives, for garnish

Directions

First of all, grease the deep dish pie plate.

Use the cooked and crumbled bacon in the bottom of pie plate.

Then use the cheese as sprinkle.

Take the eggs and mix them together with milk in bowl and then pour this mixture over cheese and bacon in plate.

Use the onions as sprinkle all over.

Then bake for approximately ½ to ¾ hour at THREE HUNDRED FIFTY (35o) degrees till set in the middle.

Then chop into wedges.

Use the sour cream and chives as garnishes.

Spicy Corn Chowder

Ingredients

2 cups fresh or frozen corn kernels

lime, juice and zest of

2 tablespoons corn oil

1 large yellow onion, peeled and minced

1 quart chicken stock, preferably homemade 2 cups peeled diced russet potatoes

1 teaspoon ground red chili powder

1/2 teaspoon crushed red pepper flakes

1 teaspoon ground cumin

1 anaheim chili, stem and pith removed, seeded and chopped 1 cup heavy cream

1/2 cup chopped fresh cilantro, plus

5 sprigs cilantro, tops for garnish

1/2 teaspoon kosher salt

garnish with drained salsa, if desired

Directions

Take the lime juice and squeeze over the corn in bowl and blend in zest and put aside.

Fry the onion in oil in saucepan over moderate temperature setting till translucent and tender.

Take stock, potato, and add them along with cumin, chili powder and red pepper flakes and heat to boiling.

Lower the temperature to moderately low, cook, covered, till potatoes become tender.

Take corn, cream and add them and keep on cooking till soup become thick.

Then add in cilantro and allow to simmer for a couple of min.

Adjust seasonings according to your own choice.

Then pour into bowls. Use cilantro sprig as garnish along with a dollop of salsa as topping over every serving.

Gold Rice with Chicken and Pistachio

Ingredients

2 teaspoons oil

1 lb boneless skinless chicken breast, cut in strips 1/2 cup chopped onion

1 cup uncooked long-grain white rice 1/2 cup shredded carrot 1/4 cup golden raisin

1 teaspoon curry powder 1 teaspoon coriander

1/4 teaspoon salt

1 (14 1/2 ounce) cans ready-to-serve chicken broth 1/2 cup water

1/4 cup shelled pistachio nut

Directions

Cook the onion and chicken strips in heated oil in skillet over moderately high temperature for FIVE min or till onion become soft and chicken become brown in color, mixing from time to time.

Add the rest of items besides nuts. Blend well.

Heat to boiling, lower the temperature to moderately low.

Cook, covered, for approximately 1/3 hour or till pink color is gone from chicken and rice become soft and liquid is assimilated.

Use the nuts as sprinkle all over.

Meat and Cheese Pie

Ingredients

1/2 lb ground beef

1/2 cup mayonnaise

1/2 cup milk

2 eggs

2 tablespoons flour

3/4 cup cheddar cheese, grated 3/4 cup cheese, grated 1/3 cup sliced green onion salt and pepper

1 9in unbaked pie shell

Directions

First of all, cook the meat in sauté pan and put aside.

Take the mayo, milk and mix them with eggs and flour till become smooth.

Blend in meat.

Blend in cheese.

Blend in onion.

Blend in salt and pepper.

Place the mixture into unbaked pie shell.

Bake for approximately FORTY min at THREE HUNDRED FIFTY (35o) degrees Fahrenheit.

Mushrooms on Toast

Ingredients

1 tablespoon extra virgin olive oil

3 -4 large fresh mushrooms, sliced

1/2 cup fat-free cottage cheese

1 tablespoon grated parmesan cheese

salt and pepper

1 slice toasted 8-grain bread or 1 slice toasted twelve-grain bread 2 teaspoons margarine

2 slices Tomatoes (thick slices)

salt and pepper

Directions

Cook the mushrooms in oil in skillet.

Then add in cottage cheese.

Use the parmesan cheese as sprinkle all over.

Then add salt as well as pepper according to your own choice and taste.

Blend and flip it to avoid sticking.

Once cottage cheese is liquid, allow to bubble for THREE min.

After this, toast the bread crunch.

Spread the little bit margarine all over.

Then put the slices of tomato over the toast.

Use salt as well as pepper as sprinkle all over.
Take mushrooms, cheese and pour them over the tomatoes.

Tasty Lasagna

Ingredients

12 ounces lasagna noodles

2 tablespoons salad oil

2 garlic cloves, minced

1 medium onion, chopped

1 lb ground beef

1 1/2 teaspoons salt

1/4 teaspoon pepper

1/2 teaspoon rosemary or 1/2 teaspoon basil 1 tablespoon parsley, minced 12 ounces tomato paste

1 1/2 cups hot water

2 eggs, beaten

1 pint cottage cheese or 1/2 lb ricotta cheese 1/2 lb mozzarella cheese, sliced 1/4 cup parmesan cheese, grated

Directions

First of all, prepare the lasagna noodles in boiling and salted water for approximately ¼ hour or till become soft.

Cook the garlic and onion in salad oil in sauté pan till tender. Then add in beef and then add in seasonings.

Cook till become crumbly.

Take tomato paste, hot water and add them.

Allow to simmer for FIVE min or put aside.

Take the beaten eggs and mix them with cottage cheese.

Put a fine layer of meat sauce in baking dish.

Then layer ½ of noodles, then layer all of cottage cheese mixture. After this, layer ½ of mozzarella, then ½ of meat sauce, remaining noodles, then remaining sauce, and then remaining mozzarella. Use the parmesan cheese as topping.

Bake for ½ hour at THREE HUNDRED FIFTY (35o) degrees Fahrenheit. Allow to cool for a couple of min prior to serving this recipe.

Dessert Meals

Pecan Pie

Ingredients

1/2-1 cup margarine

2 cups light brown sugar, packed 3 eggs

1 (9 inch) pie shells

1/4 teaspoon salt

1/2 teaspoon vanilla

1 1/2 cups pecans, chopped

Directions

First of all, add the vanilla, salt and eggs to melted margarine with sugar in saucepan.

Blend well.

Then after this, add in pecans.

Take mixture and pour this into unbaked pie shell.

Then bake for approximately ¾ hour at THREE HUNDRED FIFTY (35o) degrees Fahrenheit.

Raspberry Crisp

Ingredients

4 cups fresh raspberries, divided 3/4 cup sugar

2 tablespoons cornstarch

1 3/4 cups quick oats

1 cup flour

1 cup brown sugar

1/2 teaspoon baking soda

1/2 cup cold butter

Directions

First of all, crush one cup of berries and add water to measure ONE cup.

Take sugar and mix with cornstarch in saucepan.

Blend in raspberry mixture.

Heat to boiling and mix for 120 seconds.

Take away from heat.

Blend in rest of berries.

Allow to cool.

Take oats, flour and mix them with baking soda and brown sugar.

Chop in butter for making crumbs.

After this, press into baking dish that has been greased.

After this, spread with the berries.

Use rest of crumbs as sprinkle.

Bake for approximately ½ hour at THREE HUNDRED FIFTY (35o) degrees Fahrenheit.

Apple Dessert

Ingredients

1 yellow cake mix

1/3 cup butter, softened 1 egg

Topping

1 (21 ounce) cans apple pie filling 1/2 cup packed brown sugar 1/2 cup chopped walnuts

1 teaspoon cinnamon

1 cup sour cream

1 egg

1 teaspoon vanilla

Directions

Take cake mix, butter and blend them with egg in mixer and beat till become crumbly.

After this, press into pan.

Then after this, spread with pie filling.

Take brown sugar and mix with cinnamon and nuts.

After this, sprinkle over apples.

Take sour cream and mix with vanilla and egg in bowl.

Then after this, pour over sugar mixture.

Bake at THREE HUNDRED FIFTY (35o) degrees Fahrenheit for approximately ¾ hour or till topping become golden in color.

Marbled Style Cheesecake Brownies

Ingredients

5 tablespoons butter

2 ounces semisweet chocolate 2/3 cup sugar

2 eggs

1 teaspoon vanilla

2/3 cup flour

1/2 teaspoon baking powder Cheesecake layer

8 ounces cream cheese

1/2 cup sugar

1 egg

1 teaspoon vanilla

1 cup semisweet chocolate chips

Directions

Blend the melted butter and chocolate till become.

After this, beat in sugar.

Beat in eggs.

Beat in vanilla.

Take flour, baking powder and add them and blend them well.

Then after this, spread in baking pan that has been greased.

Then keep the cream cheese in microwave till tender and beat in sugar.

Beat in egg.

Beat in vanilla.

After this, spoon over the brownie mixture and swirl.

Use the chocolate chips as sprinkle.

Then bake for approximately ½ hour at THREE HUNDRED FIFTY (35o) degrees Fahrenheit.

Lemon Shortbread

Ingredients

1 cup all-purpose flour

1/2 cup cornstarch

1/2 cup icing sugar

2 tablespoons grated fresh lemon rind

3/4 cup butter, softened

Directions

Take flour, cornstarch and mix them with icing sugar and lemon rind in bowl.
After this, mix in butter.
Knead till soft and smooth dough is formed.
After this, roll the dough.
Chop with cookie cutters.
Put on baking sheets.
Use the colored sugars as sprinkle.

Bake for approximately 1/3 hour at THREE HUNDRED (3oo) degrees Fahrenheit or till corners become light brown in color.

Take out of sheet and allow to cool thoroughly.

Gingered Cinnamon Coffee

Ingredients

6 tablespoons ground coffee, not instant 1 tablespoon grated orange rind 1 tablespoon chopped candied ginger 1/2 teaspoon cinnamon 6 cups water

whipped cream

cinnamon stick

Directions

Take the coffee, orange peel and blend them with cinnamon and ginger.

Then place in coffee filter Then brew as instructed on the coffee maker.

Then pour into mugs.

Put cinnamon stick in every mug.

Then put a dollop of whipped cream all over.

Cream Puffs

Ingredients

1/2 cup water

1/4 cup butter or 1/4 cup margarine 1/4 teaspoon vanilla extract 1/8 teaspoon salt

7 tablespoons rice flour

2 eggs

whipped cream

Directions

First of all, heat the water, butter, salt and vanilla to boiling in saucepan over moderately high temperature setting in saucepan.

After this, put the rice flour and blend till mixture become smooth and makes a ball.

Then take away from heat.

Allow to cool for FIVE min.

Then add the eggs and beat them well till batter become smooth.

After this, drop by spoonfuls onto baking sheet.

Bake for approximately ½ hour at FOUR HUNDRED (4oo) degrees Fahrenheit or till golden brown in color and crunchy.

Allow to cool on rack.

Ice Cream

Ingredients

1/2 cup half-and-half
1 tablespoon sugar
1/4 teaspoon vanilla
1 sandwich ziploc bag
1 gallon ziploc bag
3 cups crushed ice
1/3 cup rock salt

Directions

Place 1st THREE items in small size Ziploc bag and seal it and then put ice and rock salt in large size bag and add the filled small size bag. Then finally, seal the large size bag.

After this, squeeze the bag for approximately ¼ hour or till ice cream become thick.

Take out of small bag, then unseal.

Strawberry Rhubarb Crumble

Ingredients

Topping

3/4 cup flour

2/3 cup firmly packed brown sugar 1/3 cup chopped almonds

1/2 cup butter, softened

Filling

3 pints fresh strawberries

2 lbs fresh rhubarb, cut in 1 in pieces 1 1/4 cups sugar

3 tablespoons dry tapioca

2 teaspoons freshly grated orange rind

Directions

For preparing topping, Blend everything together till mixture is crumbly in bowl.

For preparing filling, chop the strawberries and put them in large size bowl.

Blend in rest of items and allow to rest for ¼ hour.

Then butter the shallow baking dish.

Take filling and pour this into dish.

Use the topping as sprinkle.

Bake for approximately 1 hour at THREE HUNDRED FIFTY (35o) degrees Fahrenheit.

Allow to cool on wire rack.

Chocolate Zucchini Cupcakes

Ingredients

1 1/4 cups butter, softened 1 1/2 cups sugar

2 eggs

1 teaspoon vanilla extract 2 1/2 cups all-purpose flour 3/4 cup baking cocoa

1 teaspoon baking soda

1/2 teaspoon salt

1/2 cup plain yogurt

1 cup zucchini, finely grated 1 cup carrot, finely grated 16 ounces chocolate frosting

Directions

Mix the sugar and butter in bowl till fluffy.

Then add the eggs, beat well and blend in vanilla.

Take flour, baking cocoa and mix them with baking soda, salt and baking powder and then after this, add to creamed mixture alternatively with yogurt, beat well.

Then after this, fold in zucchini and fold in carrots.

Fill the muffin cups that are lined with paper.

Then bake for approximately 1/3 hour at THREE HUNDRED FIFTY (35o) degrees Fahrenheit.

Allow to cool for a couple of min.

Salad Meals

Chicken Salad

Ingredients

leftover barbecued chicken (torn or cut into bite sized bits) sliced Avocados or mango

1 -2 chopped shallots or 1/2 small red onion, finely sliced Lettuce

DRESSING enough for two chicken breasts 1/2 large lemon, juice of

1 teaspoon grainy mustard

1 tablespoon warmed honey

Directions

First of all, take the lettuce leaves and place them in a bowl and put the rest of items.

For preparing dressing, put everything in screw top jar and shake well.

After this, pour over salad.

Finally, put in fridge.

Basil & Tomato Salad

Ingredients

4 Tomatoes

1/4 cup basil leaves, torn 1 -2 tablespoon olive oil fresh ground black pepper sea salt

Directions

First of all, horizontally chop the tomatoes into slices.

Then organize on a dish.

Use the oil to drizzle and after this, scatter the basil leaves all over.

Add the salt and pepper as seasonings.

Pea Salad

Ingredients

1 (500 g) packets frozen baby peas, thawed, drained 1/2 cup finely chopped red onion 1/2 cup diced cooked bacon 1/2 cup corn kernel

1 cup grated tasty cheddar cheese 1/2 cup diced red capsicum (bell pepper) 1/4 cup sour cream

1/4 cup mayonnaise

salt & freshly ground black pepper

Directions

Blend all of the above items in a bowl.

Keep in refrigerator for chilling for a few hrs.

Creamy Feta Salad Dressing and Dip

Ingredients

5 ounces feta cheese

1/4 cup buttermilk or 1/4 cup milk 1/2 cup sour cream

1/2 cup mayonnaise

2 tablespoons white wine vinegar 2 cloves garlic, finely minced 1 green onion, finely chopped 1 teaspoon chopped fresh dill 1 teaspoon dried oregano salt and pepper

Directions

First of all, mash buttermilk and cheese together till look like the cottage cheese consistency.

Then blend in the rest of items.

After this, add the salt and pepper according to your own choice.

Allow to rest in refrigerator, covered, for a minimum of a couple of hrs.

Coleslaw

Ingredients

1/2 cabbage, shredded 1 onion, finely sliced 1 carrot, shredded

1/3 cup milk

1/2 cup mayonnaise

1/4 cup sugar

2 tablespoons vinegar 2 tablespoons lemon juice salt, pepper

Directions

Take the 1st THREE items and add them to a bowl.

Blend the rest of items in s sauce.

Then pour over the vegetables.

Blend completely and keep in refrigerator for a minimum of THREE hrs.

Potato Salad With Mustard Dressing and Bacon

Ingredients

1 1/2 cups mayonnaise

1/2 cup coarse grain mustard or 1/2 cup mustard, your favorite 1/4 cup cider vinegar

3 garlic cloves, minced

salt and pepper, to taste

1 lb bacon

5 lbs white potatoes, peeled if desired, cut into 3/4 inch pieces 4 stalks celery, sliced thin

6 green onions, sliced thin

1 1/2 cups red onions, chopped

9 hard-boiled eggs, peeled and chopped

Directions

First, take the mayonnaise, mustard and whisk them together with garlic and vinegar in a bowl.

Add the salt and pepper according to your own choice.

Then keep in refrigerator, covered.

After this, cook the bacon in sauté pan till crunchy.

Then drain them and crumble them.

After this, boil the potatoes in pot till become soft.

Then drain them and shift to bowl.

Allow to cool for ¼ hour.

Blend the eggs, red onions, green, bacon, celery, dressing into potatoes.

Add the salt and pepper if required.

Allow to chill.

Orange Romaine Salad

Ingredients

4 tablespoons red wine vinegar

3/4 cup extra virgin olive oil

1 tablespoon honey

1/2 teaspoon salt

1/4 teaspoon fresh ground black pepper 4 spring onions, sliced

1 large cos lettuce, torn into bite-size pieces 3 oranges, peeled and thinly sliced

3 tablespoons slivered almonds, toasted 2 tablespoons orange juice (optional) 1/2 teaspoon orange rind, grated very small (optional) 2 tablespoons dried cranberries (optional)

Directions

Mix the spring onion, salt, pepper, vinegar, oil, and honey in container with lid and then shake them well.

Put the cos lettuce into bowl and after this, drizzle over vinaigrette and toss them.

Then add in sliced orange and toss them.

Cheese and Green Leafy Salad

Ingredients

6 cups Lettuce, cleaned and torn

6 ounces brie cheese or 6 ounces cheese, of choice 1/4 cup lemon juice, fresh squeezed

1/4 cup extra virgin olive oil

1 lemon, zest of

Directions

First of all, distribute the greens on the four dishes.

Chop the cheese into cubes and get rid of rind and put on the greens top.

Whisk the olive oil, lemon rind and juice.

After this, take the dressing and drizzle over the greens and cheese distributing equally into FOUR dishes.

Add the salt and pepper if you like.

Pasta Salad Supreme

Ingredients

16 ounces rotini pasta or 16 ounces shell pasta 1 (8 ounce) bottles zesty dressing 4 tablespoons McCormick Salad Supreme Seasoning 5 cups assorted raw vegetables sliced olive (optional)

mozzarella cheese (optional)

Directions

First of all, cook the pasta and rinse and then drain.

Then put this pasta in salad bowl.

Add the seasoning as well as dressing.

Toss them well.

Chop the veggies into eatable pieces and then add them to pasta and blend them.

Then keep in refrigerator, covered, for a minimum of FOUR Hrs.

Easy Macaroni Salad

Ingredients

16 ounces macaroni

5 ounces tuna, drained

1 -1 1/2 cup mayonnaise, to taste 1 medium onion (peeled and finely diced) 1 carrot (peeled and shredded or grated) salt & pepper

1 -2 stalk celery (chopped)

Directions

Cook the macaroni as instructed on box and then drain the pasta and rinse with water.

Then chop the onions, carrot and celery.

After this, take the pasta, veggies, a cup of mayonnaise, tuna and add them to large size bowl.

Then use the salt and pepper for seasoning the salad.

Then keep the bowl, covered, in refrigerator till thoroughly chilled.

Appetizer Meals

Aloha Chicken Wings

Ingredients

3 lbs chicken wings

1 cup pineapple preserves

1/2 cup dry sherry

1/2 cup frozen orange juice concentrate 1/2 cup soy sauce

1/2 cup brown sugar, packed 1/4 cup vegetable oil

1 teaspoon garlic powder

1 teaspoon ground ginger

Directions

First of all, chop the wings into sections and remove the tips.

Then put these wings into resealable Ziploc bag.

Take the preserves, sherry, orange juice concentrate and blend them with garlic, ginger, oil, brown sugar and soy sauce completely.

Take the mixture and pour this over the wings in bag and seal the bag.

Then let the wings marinate, refrigerator, for SIX hrs.

Then put these wings on baking pan that has been covered with foil and pour a

cup of marinade all over wings, remove the remaining marinade.
Finally, bake for 60 min at THREE HUNDRED FIFTY (35o) degrees Fahrenheit.

Zucchini Bites

Ingredients

1 tablespoon olive oil

1 onion, finely chopped

3 slices rindless bacon, finely sliced 1 large carrot, grated

1 large zucchini, grated

3 eggs

1 cup cheese, grated

1/4 cup cream

1/2 cup self rising flour

Directions

First of all, fry the onion in oil in pan till translucent.

Take bacon and add it and sauté till begins to color.

Take zucchini, carrot and add them and cook for 120 seconds.

Then shift the mixture to bowl for cooling.

Take the cream, cheese and beat them with eggs together and add the seasoning.

Take the egg mixture and blend this into zucchini mixture.

Blend in flour.

After this, spray and flour the muffin tins and then spoon the mixture in the holes.

Finally, bake for approximately 1/3 hour at THREE HUNDRED FIFTY (35o) degrees Fahrenheit.

Maui Ahi Poke

Ingredients

2 lbs fresh ahi tuna

1 small round onion, julienne cut 3 green onions, diced

1/2 teaspoon freshly grated fresh ginger 3 finely diced garlic cloves 1/2 cup soy sauce

1 teaspoon sesame oil

1/2 teaspoon crushed red pepper flakes 1 teaspoon Chinese chili sauce 1 teaspoon sea salt or 1 teaspoon kosher salt

Directions

First of all, chop the Ahi into cubes and put aside and put in refrigerator.

Mix the rest of items in glass bowl and then keep in refrigerator for a minimum of ½ hour.

Then toss Ahi and the rest of items.

You can serve this delicious recipe with chopsticks on a dish.

Mushroom and Avocado Toast

Ingredients

2 tablespoons extra virgin olive oil

4 slices baguette or 4 slices crusty bread, 1-inch thick 1 onion, chopped

1 lb mixed mushroom, roughly chopped

2 garlic cloves, finely chopped

1 1/2 tablespoons fresh tarragon, chopped 1 Avocado, skin & stone removed, diced salt

ground black pepper

2 tablespoons parmesan cheese, freshly grated 2 tablespoons extra virgin olive oil

1 tablespoon balsamic vinegar

Directions

First of all, fry the onions in heated oil in skillet.

Then add in mushrooms. Then add in garlic.

Cook till mushrooms become wilted.

After this, take diced avocado, salt, pepper and add them.

Take away from heat once warmed.

After this, grill the sliced baguette on each of the side.

Put the toast on a dish and use the cooked mushrooms for topping.

Use little quantity of olive oil to drizzle along with balsamic vinegar.
Use the chopped tarragon and grated parmesan for topping.

Pizza Scrolls

Ingredients

1/2 small red capsicum, chopped finely 100 g ham or 100 g salami, chopped fine

1/2 cup cheese, grated

1/4 cup pizza sauce

2 sheets ready rolled puff pastry

Directions

Mix the ham, cheese and chopped capsicum in a bowl.

Take the sauce and spread this onto every pastry sheet and use the capsicum mixture as sprinkle all over.

Then roll the pastry up for enclosing the filling.

Then use the water for brushing the water and fold.

Chop every roll into ONE centimeter rounds and put them on oven trays that are lined.

And finally, bake till become golden in color.

Shrimp on the Barbie

Ingredients

1/2 cup butter, melted

1/4 cup olive oil

1/4 cup minced fresh herb, parsley and thyme 3 tablespoons fresh lemon juice 3 large garlic cloves, crushed

1 tablespoon minced shallot

salt and pepper

1 1/2 lbs shrimp, unpeeled medium to large spinach leaves (to garnish)

lemon slice (to garnish)

Directions

Mix the 1st EIGHT items in bowl. Blend in shrimp.

Allow to marinate for approximately 60 min, mixing from time to time.

After this, thread the shrimp onto skewers and grill them till become opaque, approximately 120 seconds each side.

Use the spinach for lining the dish. Then organize the skewers over the dish and use the lemon as garnish.

Barbecue Honeyed Prawns (Shrimps)

Ingredients

1 kg large raw shrimp, peeled and tails intact 2 tablespoons light soy sauce 3 teaspoons hoisin sauce 1 tablespoon barbecue sauce 1 teaspoon chili sauce

1 tablespoon honey

1 tablespoon oil

1 tablespoon dry sherry

2 cloves garlic, crushed

Directions

Mix the sherry, garlic, sauces, oil and honey in bowl. Then blend in prawns.

Then allow to marinate, covered, for 120 min.

Then grill over high temperature setting till prawns are cooked, use the marinade for brushing while you are cooking.

Honey Roasted Cashews

Ingredients

450 g unsalted cashews

2 tablespoons honey

2 tablespoons olive oil

2 teaspoons flaked sea salt

1 teaspoon cayenne pepper

Directions

Use the baking paper for lining the baking tray.

Mix the final FOUR items and pour over cashews and toss them.

Take the cashew mixture and spread over the tray Bake for TEN min at ONE HUNDRED EIGHTY (18o) degrees Fahrenheit, mixing one time or till become golden in color.

Put aside to cool and then keep in airtight container.

Deviled Scrambled Eggs

Ingredients

6 large eggs

1 tablespoon mayonnaise 1 teaspoon prepared mustard 1 tablespoon mustard pickle 1 tablespoon butter

Directions

Take the eggs, mayonnaise and beat them together with pickles and mustard.

Add the eggs to melted butter and blend to preferred doneness.

You can serve this delicious recipe with muffins.

Rimfire Cheese Balls

Ingredients

125 g Philadelphia Cream Cheese

1/2 cup tasty cheese, grated

1/4 cup parmesan cheese, freshly grated 1/2 teaspoon curry powder (or to taste)
2 tablespoons mild paprika

Directions

Mix the curry powder and cheeses in a bowl.

Then after this, add the curry powder for turning the mixture to pale yellow color.

Beat well.

Use one tbsp paprika as sprinkle all over the dish.

Roll half of the cheese mixture into a ball.

After this, take this ball and roll it in paprika.

Now put these cheese balls into plastic box, cover and keep in refrigerator, till cold.

You can serve this delicious recipe with cheese crackers.

Soup Meals

Butter Bean, Sun-Dried Tomato & Pesto Soup

Ingredients

900 ml chicken stock or 900 ml vegetable stock 2 (400 g) cans butter beans, drained & rinsed 4 tablespoons sun-dried tomato paste or 4 tablespoons sun-dried tomato puree 5 tablespoons pesto sauce

Directions

Take stock, butter beans and place them in pan and heat to boiling.

Lower the temperature. Blend in tomato puree. Blend in pesto.

Cook for FIVE min.

Then shift to food processor till become smooth and bring back to pan.

Heat, mixing from time to time, for FIVE min.

Add the seasoning.

Cream of Fish Soup

Ingredients

White Sauce

25 g butter

25 g flour

550 ml fish stock

salt

white pepper

1 garlic clove, crushed Soup

450 g cooked white fish fillets, skinned de boned, flaked 175 g peeled prawns (shrimp) salt

white pepper

75 ml cream

50 g butter

Directions

Then blend in flour in melted butter and cook for 60 seconds, after this, pour in stock and blend way from heat.

Then add the salt and pepper.

Add in crushed garlic and cover pan and allow to simmer for TEN min.

Preserve a couple of prawns for garnish, then after this, pound the remaining in mortar and pestle.

Take the fish, pounded prawns and add them to sauce and allow to simmer, covered, for next TEN min.

After this, puree soup in blender. Bring the soup back to saucepan. Adjust seasonings. Add the salt and pepper.

Take cream and add it to soup and heat again.

Use the preserved prawns as garnish.

Avocado Banana Chilled Soup

Ingredients

2 ripe Hass avocadoes, peeled, pitted and diced 2 large ripe bananas, peeled and sliced 1 cup milk

3/4-1 cup sugar

4 tablespoons lemon juice 1/2 teaspoon cinnamon

1/8 teaspoon nutmeg

1 quart plain yogurt

salt, if needed, to taste

Directions

First of all, puree the bananas and avocados in blender.

Take milk, nutmeg, yogurt, cinnamon, lemon juice, sugar and add them and mix till become smooth.

Then add in salt.

Allow to chill in refrigerator for 180 min.

Buttermilk and Shrimp Soup

Ingredients

1 quart buttermilk

1 tablespoon Dijon mustard 1 teaspoon salt

1 teaspoon granulated sugar 8 ounces cooked shrimp, chopped 1 cucumber, peeled, seeded and chopped 2 tablespoons green onions, chopped

Directions

Mix the sugar, salt, buttermilk and mustard.

Take shrimp, cucumber, green onion and add them.

Blend well.

Then keep in refrigerator, covered, for FOUR hrs.

Celery Soup

Ingredients

2 1/2 cups sliced celery

3 cups chicken stock

1 1/2 teaspoons celery salt 1/4 teaspoon nutmeg

5 teaspoons all-purpose flour 2 tablespoons milk

3 cups milk

1 cup grated cheddar cheese

Directions

Allow to simmer the stock and celery till soft.

Take celery, salt, nutmeg and add them.

Prepare paste of two tbsp of milk and flour and add to celery, mixing.

Add in three cups of milk and heat.

Then after this add in cheese.

Chiang Mai Beef Noodles

Ingredients

2 tablespoons vegetable oil

1 red onion, diced

3 garlic cloves, finely chopped

2 tablespoons curry powder

1 tablespoon red curry paste

4 cups coconut milk

500 g beef, cut into 2 . 5cm strips 1/4 cup fish sauce

2 tablespoons palm sugar

1 tablespoon lime juice

200 g fresh thin egg noodles

2 green onions, finely chopped

2 tablespoons coriander leaves

lime wedge, to serve

Directions

Sauté and mix the onion and garlic in oil in sauté pan for 60 seconds.

Take the two tbsp coconut milk, curry paste, curry powder and add them.

Sauté and mix for next 60 seconds.

Add the rest of coconut milk and allow to simmer for ½ hour.

Take the fish sauce, palm sugar, lime juice and add them.

Allow to simmer for next TEN min.

After this, take noodles and blanch them in boiling water and distribute into bowls.

After this, pour over curry mixture and use the green onions, coriander leaves and lime wedges as garnishes.

Creamy Yellow Summer Squash Soup

Ingredients

2 tablespoons butter

4 leeks, sliced

2 cups sliced summer squash 4 cups reduced-sodium chicken broth 1 cup low-fat milk or 1 cup 2% low-fat milk 1/2 teaspoon poultry seasoning salt and pepper

Directions

Fry the leeks in melted butter in saucepan over moderate temperature for FIVE min or till become tender.

Blend in a cup of broth.

Then blend in squash.

Heat to boiling.

Lower the temperature and allow to simmer till become soft.

Then shift the squash mixture to blender and puree.

Bring the puree back to saucepan and add the rest of broth and milk.

Take salt, pepper, poultry seasoning and add them according to your own choice.

And heated through.

Easy Broccoli Soup

Ingredients

1 -2 tablespoon oil

1 onion (diced)

2 garlic cloves (minced or use 2teasp from a jar) 1 large head broccoli (trimmed and chopped, about 500g) 1 potato (peeled & diced or leave skin on if you prefer) 6 cups chicken stock

salt & freshly ground black pepper 2 -3 slices bacon (diced)

Directions

Fry the garlic and onion in oil in pan over moderate temperature for THREE min or till tender.

Take stock, broccoli, potato and add them and heat to boiling.

Lower the temperature and allow to simmer for 1/3 hour or till veggies are cooked.

Blend in food processor for making smooth mixture.

Take soup and add it back to pan and heat slightly.

Then add the chopped bacon and allow to simmer till bacon is cooked, approximately ¼ hour.

Adjust seasoning.

You can serve this delicious recipe with toasted bread topped with blue cheese.

Golden Lentil Soup

Ingredients

1 cup red lentil

6 cups water

4 chicken stock cubes

4 carrots, Chopped

1 onion, Chopped

2 garlic cloves, Minced

2 teaspoons curry powder cayenne (To Taste) (optional)

Directions

Heat all of the items to boiling in pot.

Then lower the temperature.

Allow to simmer for ½ hour or till lentils become soft.

After this, puree them till become smooth.

Zucchini and Basil Soup

Ingredients

2 large onions or 2 large yellow onions or 2 large brown onions, finely chopped

2 tablespoons olive oil

2 large potatoes, peeled and cubed

750 g zucchini

salt, to taste

fresh ground black pepper, to taste

6 cups vegetable stock

1 cup basil leaves, shredded and loosely packed 4 garlic cloves, minced

2 teaspoons lemon juice

1/4 cup cream or 1/4 cup Greek yogurt

chopped parsley or shredded basil or thin slices lime, to serve

Directions

Fry the onion in pan over heat till become tender however not brown in color.

Add in potatoes and cook, covered, over gentle temperature setting.

Chop the ends from zucchinis and chop into slices and add them to pan and add in salt and ground pepper according to your own choice.

Cook, covered, for FIVE min, mixing from time to time.

Take veggie stock and add it and heat to boiling, allow to simmer, covered, for TEN min or till zucchini become soft.

Blend in basil. Blend in garlic. allow to simmer for next FIVE min.
Take away from heat and allow to cool slightly then blend the soup.
Heat again the blended soup and blend in lemon juice.
You can serve this delicious recipe with a dollop of cream.
Use chopped parsley as sprinkle along with shredded basil.

www.ingramcontent.com/pod-product-compliance
Lightning Source LLC
Chambersburg PA
CBHW081625100526
44590CB00021B/3606